# THE SHOSHONE INDIANS

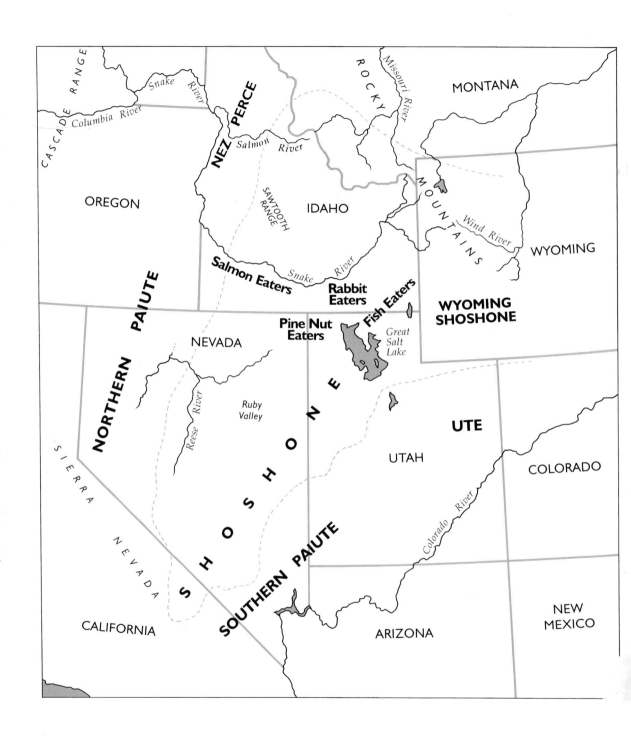

THE JUNIOR LIBRARY OF
AMERICAN INDIANS

# THE SHOSHONE INDIANS

Nathaniel Moss

CHELSEA JUNIORS
a division of CHELSEA HOUSE PUBLISHERS

FRONTISPIECE: This map shows the distribution of various Shoshone groups across the forbidding Great Basin regions of Utah, Nevada, Idaho, and Wyoming.

CHAPTER TITLE ORNAMENT: Pictograph of a lizard appearing in Native American art of the southwestern United States.

English-language words italicized in the text can be found in the glossary at the back of the book.

## Chelsea House Publishers
EDITORIAL DIRECTOR  Richard Rennert
ART DIRECTOR  Sara Davis
PICTURE EDITOR  Judy Hasday
PRODUCTION MANAGER  Pamela Loos
SENIOR PRODUCTION EDITOR  Lisa Chippendale


## Staff for THE SHOSHONE INDIANS
SENIOR EDITOR  Jane Shumate
ASSOCIATE EDITOR  Therese De Angelis
EDITORIAL ASSISTANT  Kristine Brennan
DESIGNER  Alison Burnside
PICTURE RESEARCHER  Sandy Jones
COVER ILLUSTRATOR  Shelley Pritchett

First Printing

1 3 5 7 9 8 6 4 2

Library of Congress Cataloging-in-Publication Data

Moss, Nathaniel.
The Shoshone Indians/ Nathaniel B. Moss.
p. cm.—(Junior Library of the Indians of North America)
Includes index.
Summary: Examines the history and culture of the Shoshone Indians of the Great Basin area of the United States.
   ISBN  0-7910-1674-9 (hc)
     0-7910-4625-7 (pbk)
   1. Shoshoni Indians–Juvenile literature. [1. Shoshoni Indians. 2. Indians of North America.] I. Title. II. Series.
E99. S4M67 1997
979'.004975–dc21        CIP
96-49702         AC

# CONTENTS

*The first inhabitants of the Great Basin needed to be strong and observant to find its scarce resources. This early 19th-century portrait of a Shoshone woman is by Swiss artist Karl Bodmer.*

# CHAPTER 1

# The "Unknown Land" and its People

The Great Basin is a large area in the western United States which includes all of Nevada and Utah; parts of northern Arizona and New Mexico; most of western Colorado; part of eastern California; and parts of southern Oregon, Idaho, and Wyoming. During the Ice Age, there were great mountains of ice, called glaciers, in this region. As the ice melted and formed lakes, the area could support all kinds of wildlife—even woolly mammoths. Around 10,000 B.C., however, the earth's *climate* changed. Temperatures climbed and the lakes dried up. The large animals retreated north, where temperatures were cooler, leaving behind a barren area of high mountains surrounded by valleys. The name

"Great Basin" describes the giant bowl shape formed by the valleys around the Wasatch and Sierra Nevada mountains.

Many archeologists (scientists who study bones and aritifacts to learn about the past) believe that the Shoshone's ancestors, who spoke a language called Numic, were the first people to live in the Great Basin. They think that these Numic peoples walked to the Great Basin from the Southwest about 1,000 years ago. But evidence exists to challenge that belief: archeologists have found baskets and stone tools believed to be at least 3,000 years old in the Great Basin. So it is uncertain exactly how long the Shoshone have lived there.

It is certain, however, that the Shoshone Indians were the main inhabitants of the Great Basin until the mid-1800s. They told a myth to explain how they came to live in this harsh environment. According to this story, Wolf made the earth with help from Muskrat, who brought him mud from the bottom of the sea. Wolf then created the animals and placed them in a pen, but Coyote, his mischievous younger brother, released them. It was Coyote who let people escape into the Great Basin, too. When he was given a water basket to carry across the desert—but told not to peek inside—the temptation proved too great for Coyote. Each time he lifted the lid, tiny beings hopped out of the basket. The Shoshone believe that these beings were their ancestors.

There were many different branches of the Shoshone people. The *tipatikka*, for instance, were "eaters of pine nuts." The *watatikka* were the "eaters of ryegrass seed," and the *akaitikka* were the "eaters of salmon." While the Shoshone may have been differentiated by what they ate and where they lived in the Great Basin, they shared many common characteristics that made them one people.

All of the Shoshone were *nomadic*, meaning that they survived by moving from place to place as different foods became available to them. The harsh *ecology* of their native land left them no other choice. The high mountains of the Sierra Nevada and Cascade ranges form a natural barrier to rain clouds, so the valleys of the Great Basin are very dry, receiving only about five to seven inches of rainfall per year. Temperatures also vary greatly: they can soar above 100 degrees Fahrenheit in summer and plummet below 0 degrees in winter.

Such difficult conditions required the

Shoshone to be strong and resourceful. To cope with extreme temperatures, they wore simple grass aprons in the summer and rabbit fur robes with snowshoes made out of plant fibers in winter. Shoshone women became experts at identifying edible plants. Berries, roots, seeds, and grasses were all important to their diet. Other plants had healing properties. But the most important plant resource of all was the *piñon* pine tree, which yielded seeds called pine nuts. Pine nuts were a staple of the Shoshone diet and could be prepared in a variety of ways.

The Shoshone also used inedible plants to aid in their survival. Branches and grasses were the raw material of a summer shelter called a *wickiup*: this small tent was easy to make because it consisted of just three wooden poles which were covered with dried grasses. The women wove baskets for gathering and storing food out of tough, dry sagebrush. They also discovered that by carefully coating their baskets with pine pitch—a sticky substance made from the sap of pine trees—they could make them waterproof. This knowledge was invaluable in the Great Basin, where rivers and lakes are few and far between. Shohsone men and women carried water in these special baskets (much as today's hik-

*Shoshone women made their dishes and pottery from plant fibers rather than stone or clay. Woven water carriers like this bottle were coated with pine pitch so they could hold liquids without leaking.*

ers use canteens) so they could travel great distances under the hot desert sun.

Shoshone men also used their knowledge of the land to survive. Their area of expertise was hunting. The most coveted game animal in the Great Basin was the bighorn sheep. If Shoshone hunters spotted a herd of sheep grazing near a cliff, some of them would chase the sheep over the edge while other hunters waited below to shoot them with their bows and arrows.

At other times, however, Shoshone men hunted alone and were hard-pressed to find even a single *chuckwalla*, a type of lizard. They did not have the luxury of choosing the most appetizing prey. Rats were a useful food source when big game was scarce. To catch them and other fast rodents, the Shoshone built traps. One type of trap, called a deadfall, consisted of a smooth, flat stone baited with food. The hunter would balance a heavy object on a short stick and place it next to the bait. An animal that tried to take the bait would disturb the stick—and would be crushed when the heavy object on top came crashing down. Hunters sometimes even had to content themselves with catching grasshoppers. They would carefully set fire to the underbrush or simply dig ditches around it and chase the insects out. To sustain his family in the Great Basin, a Shoshone man had to hunt any creature that was edible.

While the Great Basin's dry, forbidding ecology challenged the Shoshone people daily, it also protected them from outsiders until the 19th century. European explorers began to roam the uncharted lands of America in the 16th and 17th centuries; but even the bravest avoided the Great Basin because they considered the area too dangerous. When British and American fur trappers finally dared to enter in the 1800s, they referred to the Great Basin as the "Mysterious Land" or the "Unknown Land."

To the white people who came to this part of America, the Shoshone culture appeared primitive, and their diet of plant roots, lizards, and other wildlife seemed horrible. In 1858, J.H. Simpson, a member of the United States Army Corps of Engineers, visited the Great Basin and encountered its native people. His *prejudice* against the Shoshone was obvious when he described them as, ". . . Indians of an exceedingly low type, who subsist chiefly on roots, grass-seeds, rats, lizards, grasshoppers, etc." Many whites shared Simpson's feelings upon seeing the Indians, calling them "diggers," an insulting reference to their practice of foraging for roots.

Today, however, we realize that the Shoshone were in fact members of a highly developed civilization who understood the Great Basin well. Over many centuries, they had found a way to live in harmony with a very harsh environment. They wisely respected the limitations of the land and adapted to its conditions to get what they needed.

# CHAPTER 2

# Adapting for Survival

*Diamond Valley, Nevada, as it looks today. Despite its harsh appearance, the Shoshone called their homeland Pia Sokopia, or "Earth Mother."*

Plants and animals in the natural world are constantly adapting to their environment. The piñon pine tree so important to the Shoshone people is a good example of adaptation to the Great Basin: it needs very little water and remains fruitful for up to 400 years in a place where many other trees would surely die. Like all living things that survived in this tough environment, the people adapted, too. But unlike plants or animals, which can adapt by changing their leaves or growing fur, people usually adapt by changing their behavior.

One way the Shoshone did this was to limit the size of their family groups to no more than 20–30 people. They did this because the resources of the Great Basin were too scarce to support many people at one time. A group was made up of the members of 2 to 10 families who usually moved with each new season.

Each fall, for instance, family groups gathered near piñon pine forests to form temporary "piñon villages." These villages were groups of huts in which the people lived during the fall pine nut harvest and on through the winter. Each cone-shaped hut consisted of a ring of stones that supported poles tied together with bark, grass, and brush. The Shoshone needed fires to keep warm in winter, so each hut had an opening at the top which served as a chimney. Six or seven people could fit into a typical hut.

The pine nut was the Shoshone's most important plant food. A family of four could gather an estimated 1,200 pounds of pine nuts—four months' worth of food—during the autumn gathering season. Animals and birds also depended on the pine nut. Therefore, the people had to make sure they visited the piñon forests before their four-legged and winged neighbors picked the trees clean.

Once they had gathered the piñon tree's green cones using long, hooked harvesting poles, the Shoshone heated them in large roasting pits until they opened. They then removed the pine nuts from the opened cones and roasted them some more, until their shells were brittle enough to remove. Once shelled, pine nuts had many uses. The women ground some of them into a fine, powdery meal using a stone called a *mano*. They mixed this pine nut meal with water to make mush, which their families ate hot or cold. In freezing weather, Shoshone mothers sometimes made this mush into an ice cream-like dessert for their children.

When they were not camping in the piñon villages, groups of Shoshone visited sites where specific plant or animal resources were abundant. People of both sexes worked hard for the group's survival: men knew more about hunting, while women specialized in plant harvesting. In the spring and summer, Shoshone women gathered seeds, roots, berries, and leaves. Over 100 varieties of plants were useful— some as food or medicine, others as the raw materials of shelters, tools, and baskets.

Shoshone women were proud of the baskets they wove. Each type of basket had its own special purpose and shape: there was the gathering basket, the burden basket, the berry basket, and the water-carrying basket. The women decorated them with geometric designs, which they either painted on with vegetable dyes or wove into the basket with dyed plant fibers. These ornamented baskets were valuable in trade with other native peoples. Shoshone women traded them for beautiful seashells, which they used to make earrings and necklaces.

The women used curved hardwood digging sticks to gather camas (the edible roots of the lily plant), swamp onions, and valerian, all of which could be eaten raw or cooked. Shoshone in the northern part of the Great Basin were especially involved in the spring harvest of roots such as tampa, bitterroot, and biscuitroot. Berries and fruits, on the other hand, were important to Shoshone throughout the Great Basin. Women and children collected berries in baskets they hung around their necks. When those baskets were full, they would transfer the berries into larger baskets, which they wore like backpacks.

The Shoshone also harvested leaves, which they either boiled, ate raw, or dried to make medicinal teas. They peeled the

*The large, edible seeds of the piñon pine tree (left) were so important to the Shoshone that they camped in piñon forests at harvest time. Men, women, and children once collected pine nuts in cone-shaped carrying baskets like this one (right).*

husks off of cattail and thistle to eat the watery *pith* inside. A snack of raw mesquite pods was a springtime treat. By late summer, however, the mesquite pods had dried enough to be ground into meal. Women ground the pods in hard wooden or stone bowls called *mortars*. Mesquite meal was used as a flour for sweet cakes, which were made by mixing the meal with the syrupy extract of cooked agave leaves.

Shoshone women used plants for more than making sweets, though. Many were skilled *herbalists*—people who used plants to treat illness. These herbalists were considered the equals of men. More than 300 medicinal plants were known to the herbalists. For instance, cedar pitch helped cuts heal; the Oregon grape was useful in treating eye ailments; snakeweed soothed upset stomachs.

Not to be outdone by the women, Shoshone men were clever and skillful hunters. They made their own knife blades and arrowheads. Hammering a stone until it broke into a sharp point then shaping it into an arrowhead took an experienced man about 20 minutes. The men also knew how to sharpen knives by running their blades across a piece of antler or horn. These handmade weapons were more sophisticated than they looked: arrowheads were often dipped in a poison such as rattlesnake venom or a deadly plant extract to give the hunters an added edge.

The men hunted alone or in groups for bighorn sheep, which roamed widely over the Great Basin. A man might shoot one with his bow and arrow by waiting along its favorite trails. In rutting season, male bighorn sheep (or rams) competed for mates by butting each other with their long, curved horns. To trick them, Shoshone hunters disguised themselves in the skin and horns of a sheep. By beating on logs to imitate the sounds of a rutting battle, the men attracted the sheep towards their waiting arrows. This method also worked for mule deer and pronghorn antelope, two other big game animals of the Great Basin. Groups of Shoshone hunters would sometimes chase herds of these animals into natural canyons or into pits that they dug themselves.

A large animal like a bighorn sheep, mule deer, or pronghorn antelope was hard to catch, though. Rabbits were a more common source of meat and warm fur for winter robes. Scientists have found centuries-old dog remains together with those of people in the Great Basin, so the Shoshone probably used domesticated dogs to help in the hunt. Women and children also helped in rabbit hunts by flushing rabbits out of hiding in the sagebrush, then chasing them towards the waiting nets of the men. The men killed the rabbits with clubs or arrows before the animals became entangled in the nets, which were hard to repair.

Small birds could also be captured with nets. To hunt ducks, however, the Shoshone used decoys. These lures were suprisingly lifelike: the skin and feathers of real ducks were stretched over frames made out of reeds. An especially crafty hunter might wait for his decoys to attract ducks to a river or lake, then lurk underwater himself until he could grab a bird by its legs and drown it. Men, women, and children alike collected bird eggs. They could be stone-boiled (boiled in water with heated rocks added to it) or kept fresh by burying them in the cool ground.

Men sometimes used nets to catch fish. But they also built fence-like traps called *weirs*, which closed off whole sections of rivers so that they could harpoon the fish. The Shoshone knew that weirs were especially useful for catching salmon as they migrated from the Pacific ocean to spawn (lay eggs). The Snake River and its tributaries were particularly important sources of salmon for the Shoshone.

Women prepared the fish and game that men killed. They barbecued meat over open flames or filled the cleaned body cavities of large animals with water, then added red-hot stones to cook them from within. Women also prepared some meat so it would stay fresh on long trips by drying it, then grinding it together with a mixture of berries and fat. This high-energy food, called *pemmican*, was also eaten by Indians of many other tribes.

However much the first Europeans to meet the Shoshone may have disdained their way of life, it was clear that these native people deeply appreciated the land. "They are lovers of their country; lovers not of fair hills and fertile valleys, but of inhospitable mountains and barren plains," wrote historian Hubert Howe Bancroft in 1883.

Indeed, the Shoshone tried not to waste anything they killed or harvested. They also knew that after they hunted a particular animal, they had to allow its population time to recover. In their religion, the spirits who inhabited the earth and the sky would reward them with a plentiful food supply if they treated nature's resources with respect. Nature, the spirit world, and the Shoshone were tied together by the circle of life. ▲

# CHAPTER 3

# The Circle of Life

The Great Basin provided three things for the Shoshone: food, shelter, and a basis for their spiritual life. It was Wolf who created the world, but it was Coyote who insisted that all living things take part in the cycle of life and death. The people tried to be aware of their place in the circle of life at all times. They took what they needed from the land but always gave thanks to the spirit world for making life possible. The Shoshone believed that they were in constant communication with spirits. Coyotes and wolves, piñon trees and sagebrush, rivers and mountains, and even the stars had *supernatural* powers that could help or hurt them.

The nature spirits could do harm if the people ignored them, but the Shoshone also believed that they could be powerful allies if shown proper respect.

Performing rituals was an important way of showing respect. The people marked important events like births, marriages, and deaths with elaborate ceremonies in which they gave thanks to nature for their place in the circle of life. They also performed rituals to ask for help in getting what they needed from the challenging world in which they lived.

Shoshone hunters and warriors asked the spirit world for success in the hunt and in battle. In return for this help, the men gave thanks. The people always showed their respect for the animals and plants they depended upon for survival. In fact, among some speakers of the Shoshone language today, Coyote is still called "our father's brother," Bear is "our father's sister," and Rattlesnake is known as "our father's father."

The underlying philosophy of Shoshone religion was that respect for the spirit world would be rewarded by good fortune. When a bighorn sheep or pronghorn antelope was killed, for example, hunters would place the slain animal's head to the east (the source of the rising sun), and later offer its skull and eyes back to the spirit world. During future hunts, the animal's blood might be sprinkled onto the tracks of a deer or sheep. The Shoshone believed that the blood would magically weaken game animals, making them easier to catch.

Some hunting parties were lucky enough to have a member who possessed special power. These men were called *shamans*, and they might have the power to envision the best hunting grounds in their dreams, or to hear instructions from nature spirits. They usually received their powers during a ritual called the *vision quest*. During a vision quest, a young Shoshone man would go out into the wilderness alone, naked except for a blanket. He would abstain from eating or drinking and bathe in a creek or lake to purify himself. Then the youth would wait for the spirits to contact him: this contact might take the form of lightning, a strong wind, or birds circling overhead.

But the spirits might test his courage by sending a rattlesnake or a coyote. When his personal spirit finally contacted him, it could appear as a person or an animal—or be heard as a soft voice on the wind. The spirit would give the vision seeker special powers. For instance, a beaver spirit might give his Shoshone brother great swimming

ability, or an antelope spirit might endow him with swiftness.

With the young man's new gift came responsibility, though. He might be instructed to wear feathers, a deer tail, or an antelope hoof. He might have to learn a sacred song. The vision seeker listened carefully to

*Drawing of Tsoavits, the man-eating ogre believed by the Shoshone to eat anyone unlucky enough to be caught in his giant carrying basket.*

his spirit guide: breaking any of its rules would result in a loss of his new power—or worse. He might be punished with bad luck, an accident, or a sickness.

Some shamans received the power to cure illness on their vision quests. Whites called these people "medicine men," but the Shoshone called them *puhagan*, the possessors of power, or *puha*. They would treat those patients who did not respond to an herbalist's cures. The puhagan would perform sacred *incantations* as part of their healing rituals.

Vision seekers who were taught songs and incantations had to memorize them faithfully, because the Shoshone people had no written language. They passed their knowledge about the spirit world from generation to generation through storytelling. The elders told children about Wolf, Coyote, and the circle of life. They told tales of magic and courage—and stories which taught children lessons about proper behavior. A culture in which people memorize stories to tell their children and grandchildren is said to have an *oral tradition*.

One scary story in the Shoshone's oral tradition is that of *Tsoavits*, a giant ogre who roamed the Great Basin. He lived in the Sawtooth Mountains of south central Idaho.

The Shoshone called this area *coapiccan kahni*, or "the giant's house." It was said that Tsoavits could paralyze a person with one terrifying glance. Then the giant would catch his helpless victim with the same type of hook that Shoshone hunters used to catch chuckwalla lizards and place him or her in a basket just like the women's carrying baskets. Tsoavits would take those he captured back to his house and eat them. The people believed that the only way to kill Tsoavits was by burning him.

As children grew up, there were rituals surrounding important *rites of passage*, or transitions into the next stage in life. The leap to manhood for Shoshone boys was marked by the first vision quest. When girls became women, they were isolated from their families and neighbors in small sagebrush lodges. After a ritual cleansing ceremony, the girls put on new clothes and reentered the community as women ready for husbands.

Marriage was vital to the Shoshone's survival since most men hunted and most women harvested plants. Only by cooperating could people get what they needed from the harsh terrain of the Great Basin. Most people could only afford to keep one spouse, but on rare occasions a man would marry two sisters. In places where men out-numbered women, a wife might have more than one husband. The winter piñon villages were good places to find marriage partners. There, young men and women had a chance to meet, play, and dance together in the celebrations that followed the pine nut harvest.

Dancing was important to the Shoshone for both social and spiritual reasons. A favorite dance was the *natayati*, which meant "lifting the feet together." It was a round dance, in which the entire Shoshone community joined in a circle. The dancers moved to the music of drums, rasps, rattles, and flutes. Everyone sang songs led by a round dance poet, or *hupiakanti*.

When a Shoshone couple was expecting a child, both husband and wife observed ritual *taboos*. These were rules of behavior that would ensure a healthy baby. The man and the woman avoided fatty foods and drank plenty of hot water to make sure that the child would not be lazy and that the mother would have an easy labor. A Shoshone mother gave birth in a small lodge with help from a midwife, an herbalist who specialized in assisting childbirth. The newborn baby was washed in warm water. Mother and child lived apart from the rest of their village for one month, then underwent a purification ritual before rejoining the group.

Shoshone children were rarely punished. Instead, they learned to be disciplined workers by helping out with chores almost as soon as they were able to walk. Very young children gathered fruits, leaves, and seeds with their mothers. As they grew, youngsters helped chase rabbits during the group hunts and raided eggs from birds' nests.

Childhood was not all work, though. Young Shoshone played one game in which they rolled a hoop over the ground by guiding it with a stick. Though their main concern was having fun, the children who played this game also trained themselves to run great distances without tiring—a valuable survival skill. Other playtime activities were more directly related to adult skills. Shoshone girls played string games like cat's cradle, which prepared them to weave baskets and nets in the future. Boys held archery contests and began to hunt small animals at an early age.

Although there was time for play, Shoshone childhood was not carefree. Being part of the circle of life meant witnessing death, too. When someone in their community died, the Shoshone believed

*(continued on page 37)*

## FACING CHANGE THROUGH ART

Although they spent much of their time roaming the Great Basin in search of food and water, the Shoshone also expressed themselves artistically. Everyday items, such as woven plant fiber baskets, were often adorned with geometric designs. When white homesteaders forced the Shoshone to share their reservation land with the Sioux and the Arapaho, they managed to live peacefully among their old enemies. This successful blending of the tribes can be seen in Shoshone crafts made during the early reservation years. Although their designs were inspired by neighboring tribes, the Shoshone's art helped them retain their Indian identity—even as the government tried to force them to live like whites.

*Soft-soled moccasins with floral beadwork became popular among native groups west of the Rockies during the early reservation years. The design on the top of these women's moccasins is called a "Shoshone Rose."*

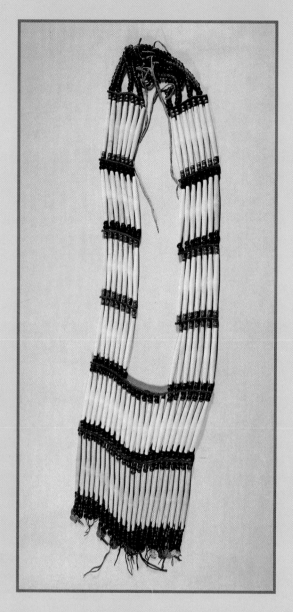

This women's breastplate is made from alternating rows of hairpipes and beads strung together on rawhide. The tapering, columnar hairpipes are so called because they were once used as hair ornaments. The Shoshone first made hairpipes from conch shells obtained through trade with West Coast tribes; later, an enterprising trader set up a New Jersey factory to make copies from bone. This style of breastplate, with its red and green cut glass beads, was popular among the Shoshone of the late 1890s.

The baby carriers of the Shoshone, Flathead, and Kutenai tribes consisted of animal skins sewed onto tapering, elongated slats that came to a rounded top. This toy carrier is scaled down to carry a little girl's doll. The flat, neat stitchery and the choice of colors on this example are characteristic of the work of Shoshone craftswomen at the turn of this century.

Eagle-feather headdresses are closely associated with Plains tribes. This Shoshone headdress was made around the turn of this century, when military native groups had all but died out. The privilege of wearing a headdress was originally reserved for revered leaders in battle: this one probably belonged to an elderly former warrior.

This large envelope-shaped parfleche is made of painted rawhide. The Shoshone and other nomadic Plains tribes usually made them in pairs to store their belongings on each side of a saddle.

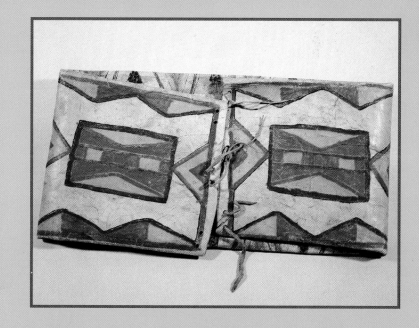

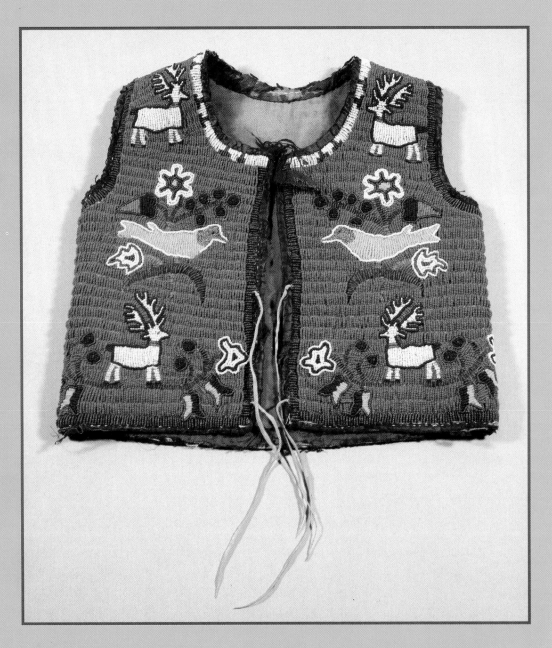

*Euro-American vests were interpreted imaginatively by Native Americans. Indian men began wearing commercial cloth vests in the 1870s, and, by the end of the 19th century, Shoshone women on reservations began cutting simple leather vests and decorating them with beadwork. This example, adorned with two elk to symbolize strength and power, is typical of that period.*

*This Shoshone woman wears a dress studded with elk teeth. Clothing sometimes symbolized important life changes. When girls became women, for example, they wore new clothes to signal their readiness for marriage. And after loved ones died, people put on new outfits after their period of mourning ended.*

*(continued from page 32)*

that the person's spirit went on to a world of peace and prosperity. They painted the body with red and white stripes and buried it along with items the person had valued in life. These things might be weapons for a man; for a woman, they could be baskets.

The grave was covered with large stones to protect it from wild animals and the people observed two days of mourning. During this time, the Shoshone burned sagebrush to hasten the dead person's ghost on to the next world and to protect the living from evil spirits.

For the dead person's family, however, the period of grief lasted for six months. Women in mourning might slash their arms and legs with knives. They also cut their hair so short that it only reached their ears. Men cut their long hair to shoulder length. People of both sexes wore the same clothes every day while in mourning. After six months had passed, family members painted themselves red and donned new clothing. The community joined the mourners in a round dance and encouraged them to give up their sadness.

All of these rituals—of birth, growing up, marriage, and death—were parts of the Shoshone circle of life. For many centuries, the people lived this way without interruption. But the discovery of America by the Spanish—and the English and French explorers that soon followed—would change the Shoshone's lives forever. Their remote, treacherous location would protect them until after the *Louisiana Purchase.*

President Thomas Jefferson bought the land stretching from present-day Oregon in the north to what is now Louisiana. He was not sure of exactly what he had acquired from the French emperor, Napoléon Bonaparte, so he sent a scouting party to explore the unknown land. This party was led by two men, Meriwether Lewis and William Clark. To help them navigate this uncharted land, Lewis and Clark relied on a Shoshone Indian. Her name was Sacajawea. ▲

*Sacajawea, a Shoshone, became an important figure in American history when she guided the Lewis and Clark expedition through her childhood home in present-day Montana.*

# CHAPTER 4

# Sacajawea, the Guide

Europeans arrived in North America long before they came into contact with the Shoshone. Spanish *conquistadors* toppled the Aztec civilization of Mexico in 1521. They then moved north, bringing with them guns and iron tools to trade with the native peoples they met. But one thing about the Spanish conquest of America would change native culture more than tools or guns: the Spaniards came on horseback.

The Plains Indian tribes were the first native people to take advantage of the horse. Horses were helpful in flat, grassy areas like the Great Plains. Mounted warriors could surprise their enemies, then get away quickly. Hunters on horseback could follow great herds of buffalo without getting tired. This ensured them plenty of meat, shelter, and clothing. Thanks to horses, native groups living east of the Rocky Mountains, such as the Sioux and the Cheyenne, grew into great military powers after 1700.

For most Shoshone, however, horses would have actually made life more difficult. They competed with people for the few grasses that grew in the Great Basin. Hunting small game like rabbits was actually easier on foot than on horseback, and the Shoshone did not need horses to harvest pine nuts. In the heart of the Great Basin— where even horses could not travel easily— the people continued their traditional way of life, foraging and hunting on foot.

But some Shoshone did benefit from the arrival of horses. For those living on the eastern edge of the Great Basin, the land closest to the Rocky Mountains was grassy enough to make owning horses practical. Some of these Shoshone even formed an entirely new tribe, the Comanche. They migrated into present-day Wyoming, then traveled south to the Plains, where they became great riders and horse breeders. Another Shoshone group who used horses lived in the northernmost part of the Great Basin. They banded with Northern Paiute Indians to form the Bannock Shoshone tribe.

It was in Bannock Shoshone territory that a girl named Sacajawea was born around 1788. She was born in the western Rocky Mountains, a few miles east of the Salmon River in what is now Idaho. When she was 10 years old, Sacajawea traveled to an area known as Three Forks near the present-day city of Bozeman, Montana. One day, the Shoshone camp at Three Forks was raided by warriors from the Minitari tribe. Sacajawea, who had been picking berries with the other women and children, was captured and forced to live as a Minitari slave. Sacajawea lived among the Minitari for several years. Though she learned their language, she never forgot her own. When she was 15 years old, a French Canadian man named Toussaint Charbonneau bought Sacajawea from the Minitari chief. He also acquired another Shoshone wife, who was called Otter Woman.

At about the same time, Lewis and Clark began their expedition. They set off from St. Louis along the Missouri River. President Jefferson sent them with the hope that they might find a water route leading all the way to the Pacific Ocean. Jefferson eagerly looked forward to the day when the United States would reach from the Atlantic Ocean in the east to the Pacific in the west. This idea that America would inevitably take up the whole continent is called manifest destiny.

The boats of the Lewis and Clark expedition were called the Corps of Discovery. Meriwether Lewis was the captain of the fleet. President Jefferson instructed him to treat the native peoples he met in a friendly manner. Lewis and Clark agreed, because they realized that they would need the help of people who knew the territory. Before they left, the explorers bought firearms, scientific instruments, food, and some of the first matches ever made. They spent $2,000 (an enormous sum of money at the time) for these gifts, which were intended for the Native Americans they would encounter on their journey.

By winter, the Corps of Discovery arrived in North Dakota—home of the Mandan Indians. Living among the Mandan were Toussaint Charbonneau, Sacajawea, and Otter Woman. As the explorers made camp for winter, they planned their trip to the West Coast. Crossing the Rocky Mountains would

*Karl Bodmer's depiction of a buffalo hunt. Because the dry interior of the Great Basin supported little grass for grazing, only the Shoshone living on the edge of the Great Plains became mounted hunters and warriors.*

require horses.  Lewis and Clark learned that the group with horses living closest to the Rocky Mountains were Shoshone. To communicate with them, the men would need an interpreter: Sacajawea, a native speaker of the Shoshone language, was their choice. Lewis and Clark convinced Charbonneau and Sacajawea to come west with them. Otter Woman would remain with the Mandan.

Over the winter, Sacajawea gave birth to a baby boy named Jean-Baptiste. Her labor was difficult, but Captain Lewis, who had some medical training, was able to ease her pain with opium. She was also given a few rings of a rattlesnake's tail—a native remedy. When spring came, Sacajawea strapped Jean-Baptiste to her back and accompanied the fleet down the Missouri River to a place where three rivers met. Sacajawea recognized it as Three Forks, the camp from which she had been kidnapped as a child.

Sacajawea also remembered that her people used to fish in a river that ran slightly west of Three Forks. Captain Lewis set off with a small scouting party and soon met some Shoshone women. Lewis painted the Indians' faces with a red dye—a sign of peace, according to Sacajawea. He also gave them beads as presents. The women led Lewis and his party to a large group of Shoshone warriors, whose leader was a man named Cameahwait.

Captain Lewis made it very clear to Cameahwait that his intentions were peaceful. He presented the Indians with a flag. They in turn shared a peace pipe with the strangers. Cameahwait and the other

Shoshone chiefs followed Captain Lewis to the Corps of Discovery's camp. After sharing another peace pipe, Lewis brought Sacajawea into the group to interpret. Upon seeing Cameahwait, she cried out in joy and disbelief: he was her brother!

She also met the Shoshone man who would have been her husband had she not been kidnapped. He had given Sacajawea's father a gift of horses when she was a little girl to secure her hand in marriage when she grew up. Upon seeing that Sacajawea and Charbonneau had a child together, he gave up his claim to her, and Sacajawea decided to stay with the Corps of Discovery.

Once the excitement subsided, Lewis asked the Shoshone to lend him 30 horses and a guide. Negotiations were complicated: Cameahwait spoke to Sacajawea in Shoshone, and Sacajawea translated the chief's words into Minitari for Charbonneau, who then communicated with Lewis and Clark in French and English. Finally, with Sacajawea's encouragement, Cameahwait agreed to give them the horses and the guide.

But the Shoshone also told the explorers that they knew of no water route to the Pacific. An older Shoshone man called Toby spoke of a water route to the north, however. Toby and his four sons became guides

for the expedition. It took two weeks of very difficult travel to reach Lolo Creek, which lay just south of present-day Missoula, Montana. (Today the same trip takes only three hours by car.)

By the time the explorers reached Lolo Creek, they had eaten all of their food. Some of Lewis and Clark's men tried to hunt without success. When they finally killed a horse to eat, Sacajawea and the other horrified Shoshone refused to join them. Finally, the party descended from the Rocky Mountains and arrived in Weippe Prairie,

*Meriwether Lewis (left) and William Clark were instructed by President Thomas Jefferson to treat all native peoples they met in a friendly manner. But the purpose of the Lewis and Clark expedition was to help open the West to white settlement—which would soon put an end to the Shoshone's nomadic way of life.*

Idaho. They camped near the Nez Perce Indians, who treated them to a feast of salmon, buffalo, and camas.

The chief of the Nez Perce was a man named Twisted Hair. He drew a map for Lewis and Clark. They could reach the Pacific by following three rivers. The first one, the Clearwater, would take them to the Snake River. The Snake River emptied into the Columbia River, which ran all the way to the Pacific. The Nez Perce offered them three guides; Toby and his sons returned to the Shoshone.

As the expedition traveled down the Snake River, they passed groups of Native Americans fishing for salmon. The presence of Sacajawea among the white explorers helped calm any fears that the Indians had. As William Clark noted in his diary, "A woman with a party of men is a token of peace." They soon reached the Columbia River, along which they continued to see more native groups. On one occasion, Clark shot at a duck, apparently scaring the Indians on the riverbank. But again, the reassuring presence of Sacajawea kept things calm. Clark noted, "No woman ever accompanied a war party in this quarter."

There were many waterfalls along the rivers. Each time the explorers came to one, they had to paddle their canoes to shore. Standing on dry land, they would lower the canoes down the waterfall using ropes made out of braided elk skin. On November 7, 1805, the party glimpsed their destination: the Pacific Ocean. Clark's diary entry captures the expedition's high spirits: "O the joy! That ocean, the object of all our labors, the reward of all our anxieties. The cheering view exhilarated the spirits of all the party, who were still more delighted on hearing the distant roar of the breakers."

After their successful journey to the Pacific, Lewis and Clark prepared to return to Washington, D.C. They hoped to find trading vessels at the mouth of the Columbia River, so they could return by sea. Much to their disappointment, no boats awaited them. The party camped for the winter. The following spring, they returned the way they had come by land. On the return trip, Sacajawea and Charbonneau decided to stay with the Mandan.

While Charbonneau was paid for his services, Sacajawea was not. But William Clark did give Charbonneau a note which said, "This man has been very serviceable to us, and his wife was particularly useful among the Shoshones. Indeed, she has borne with a patience truly admirable the fatigues of so long a route encumbered with the charge of an infant who is even now only nineteen months old."

Lewis and Clark made their report to President Jefferson. Maps were drawn of the territory they had explored. Ten territories were identified: the future states of Missouri, Kansas, Nebraska, Iowa, South Dakota, North Dakota, Montana, Idaho, Oregon, and Washington.

Through Sacajawea, the Shoshone Indians participated in one of the most important adventures in United States history.

Unfortunately, the work of Lewis and Clark also paved the way for wagons full of land-hungry settlers to invade the American West. The stage was set for a grim new chapter in the history of the Shoshone people. ▲

# CHAPTER 5

# America Moves West

*A Mormon wagon train heads west into the Great Basin. The first Mormon settlers in Shoshone territory, who arrived in 1847, sought to convert the tribe peacefully.*

The late 18th century heralded the end of life as the Shoshone knew it. The Spanish brought more than horses to the western United States: they also brought guns. With guns they could enslave native peoples or even pay tribes to provide them with slaves from among their enemies. But Spanish slave traders were not alone in threatening the future of the Shoshone. They would soon see fur traders, then religious refugees, miners, and other white explorers make their way into the Great Basin. Over the next 50 years, this influx of settlers would change their way of life forever.

Fur trappers first came to the Great Basin in large numbers during the 1820s. To get Congress to approve the Lewis and Clark expedition, President Jefferson pointed out that better knowledge of the western United States would help American fur traders compete with the British. Jedediah Smith crossed into central Nevada in 1827. He was sent by the Rocky Mountain Fur Company in search of beavers. Although unsuccessful in his quest, he met many of the Shoshone. He described them as, ". . . the most miserable of the human race having nothing to subsist on (nor any clothing) except grass seeds, grasshoppers, etc."

From 1828–1829, Peter Skene Ogden of the British Hudson's Bay Company led a party of fur trappers to the Humboldt River in present-day Nevada. They trapped so many beavers there that they deprived the local Shoshone of the fur they needed for their winter clothing. To make matters worse, Ogden's livestock ate precious grasses that the Indians used for food. The Shoshone referred to the whites as *taipo*, and were angry that they were destroying the land. Sadly, this was just a hint of things to come.

Within 15 years, the fur trade ended because the beaver population had been

The Shoshone helplessly watched whites invade their ancestral home as railroad tracks extended into the Great Basin. This photograph shows the Transcontinental Railroad being built near Wyoming's Green River during the winter of 1867–68.

trapped to extinction. The out-of-work trappers now offered their knowledge of the Great Basin to mapmakers who were looking for a land route to the Pacific coast. At first, explorers sought a water route—the legendary Buenaventura River. But John C. Frémont, an engineer for the United States Army, proved that the Buenaventura did not exist. He was so highly respected for his explorations that he became known as "the Great Pathfinder." He considered the land of the Great Basin worthless, and wrote that the Shoshone were "the nearest approach to the mere animal creation."

Frémont did not appreciate the many survival tactics the people had developed to take advantage of scarce resources. Even worse, however, explorers like Frémont did not value the land because it was not suitable for growing crops like wheat, barley, and rye. As Frémont and others passed through the Great Basin, their horses ate all of the grasses. Diseases spread by European livestock killed many of the rabbits that supplied the Shoshone with fur and meat. Furthermore, the settlers themselves carried diseases that killed many native people. And the sound of European firearms scared game out of shooting range for Shoshone hunters armed with bows and arrows.

Slowly but surely, their traditional forms of subsistence were being destroyed. One of Frémont's mapmakers wrote, "The white people have ruined the country of the Snake (Shoshone) Indians and should therefore treat them well. Almost all the natives are now obliged to live on roots, game can scarcely be seen anywhere."

Some of the Shoshone fought back by stealing livestock from the white intruders. But this practice was dangerous: sometimes Indian men were shot and killed by whites during their raids. On other occasions, the Shoshone scavenged among leftover food abandoned by traveling whites.

In 1847, a new group of white settlers made their way to the Great Basin in search of religious freedom. They followed a leader named Brigham Young and they called themselves Mormons. They settled in the Salt Lake Valley of Utah. Their goal was to begin a new Mormon country called Deseret. Their founder, a man named Joseph Smith, had been murdered the previous year.

The land that the Mormons settled in was Mexican territory at the time. They assumed they would be left in peace. They would have been right, were it not for the 1848 Treaty of Guadelupe Hidalgo. In this treaty, Mexico ceded its land in the Great Basin to the United States. When gold was discovered in California during the same year, thousands of Americans flooded into the Great Basin area. In 1849, some 25,000 gold miners crossed into this territory.

The Mormons clashed with the gold miners over how to treat native peoples. The Mormons respected the Shoshone: they hoped to one day convert them to the Mormon faith. The miners, on the other hand, distrusted them—just as they did most Native Americans. This conflict deepened. In 1857, miners in a wagon train headed for California were ambushed and killed by a group of Mormons as they passed through Utah. This grisly episode became known as the Mountain Meadows Massacre.

The gold rush intensified in 1859 when the Comstock Lode (an underground vein of silver and gold) was discovered in Nevada. Still more prospectors made their way into the Great Basin, stripping the land of resources as they went. Things got even worse for the Shoshone with the outbreak of the Civil War in 1861. The Pony Express and telegraph lines were routed through their territory. These developments brought even more whites to the West. White settlers often told exaggerated stories about run-ins with murderous Indians to enhance their own reputations. In 1861, a Bannock Shoshone chief named Pocatello was accused of leading a war party that killed 300 white travelers at Almo, Idaho. Two years later, Colonel Patrick Edward Connor sought revenge by leading an attack on a Shoshone camp. Connor's campaign, known as the Battle of Bear River, ended the lives of 250 Shoshone—many of them women and children.

But of all the sudden changes they faced, the building of mines had the greatest impact on the Shoshone. When mining began at the Comstock lode, the surrounding moutains were covered with piñon and juniper. Less than a decade later, in 1868, there were 24 sawmills in Nevada. These mills produced as much lumber to build underground mine shafts in the Great Basin as had been used to build the entire city of Chicago! When the piñon trees were chopped down, the Shoshone tribe lost one of their most important resources— and worse, an impor-

*A Shoshone warrior, believed to be a member of Pocatello's band. Pocatello was a Bannock Shoshone chief who was accused in 1861 of leading an attack that killed 300 whites as they passed through Idaho.*

tant part of their spiritual life.

As mining towns grew, farmers and cattle ranchers came to the new territory. The ranchers' herds ate up still more of the precious grass upon which the Shoshone depended. The European style of agriculture did great damage to the land: valleys were plowed for crops or used as pasture for livestock.

These changes profoundly affected the ecology of the region. Cattle and other livestock ate the plants that prevented soil erosion, so foothills quickly turned into dust. White settlers grew new types of plants which soon crowded out the old. Rabbits and birds fed on the white farmers' crops. The farmers considered these small animals to be pests and shot them, further reducing the Shoshone's food supply. A species of domestic fish called the German carp was introduced into local streams. The carp fed on aquatic plants that water birds depended on.

The white settlers farmed and hunted without regard for their environment. They may have called the Shoshone "primitive," but it was they who were backward. Bighorn sheep were hunted heavily, but not given time to repopulate. Overfishing and the construction of dams deprived the Shoshone of salmon.

In the end, the Shoshone were forced to begin working for wages. They took jobs on farms, in mines, and at lumber mills. Captain Sam, a Shoshone chief, explained to a federal Indian agent in 1870 that, ". . . the game were all gone; the trees that bore pine nuts were cut down and burned in the quartz-mills and other places; the grass seeds, heretofore used by them for food, were no more, the grass land all claimed by and cultivated by the white people; and that . . . Indians would soon be compelled to work for the ranches for two bits a day or starve." The Shoshone could no longer live off their land. They could either work for the white settlers or perish.

But the U.S. government offered them another option by setting aside tracts of land for them. In the years to come, thousands of Shoshone would try to reclaim their old way of life on these *reservations*. Some of them were forced to relocate; others, like the Eastern Shoshone under the leadership of their chief, Washakie, wanted a reservation. In 1855, Washakie articulated his peoples' inability to live as they used to when he said, "Since the white man has made a road across our land and has killed off our game, we are hungry, and there is nothing for us to eat. Our women and children cry for food and we have no food to give them." But Washakie and the rest of the Shoshone would discover that even on the reservations, their traditional culture was not safe. ⧗

*Chief Washakie sits for a photograph on the Wind River Reservation. In his old age, Washakie foresaw the pointlessness of fighting white settlement and asked the federal government to set aside land for his Eastern Shoshone followers.*

# CHAPTER 6

# Loss and Renewal

Between 1839 and 1868, the lands of the Great Basin were divided into United States Territories. Within these territories reservations were set aside for native peoples. The government said this would help the Indians become self-sufficient farmers and ranchers. But the Shoshone already knew more about self-sufficiency than whites could ever teach them. The real reason the government set up the reservations was to make it easier to establish mines and farms by getting Indians out of the way.

Agents from the Bureau of Indian Affairs

(BIA) were asked by the U.S. government to help decide where the reservations should be established. Between 1852 and 1904, these federal agents made almost 25 treaties with the Shoshone. Federal agents made separate treaties with each group. Among these groups were the Eastern Shoshone, the Western Shoshone, and the Northern Shoshone.

It was bad enough that the white settlers in the Great Basin had depleted the Shoshone's land of resources; now they began stealing it. For example, a treaty in 1863 gave the Northern Shoshone and Bannock Indians the rights to the Kamas Prairie in Idaho. In the treaty, the word "Kamas" was misspelled as "Kansas." This mistake allowed white settlers to legally ignore Indian claims to the land. Another treaty with the Western Shoshone was disregarded by local miners.

In 1868, Chief Washakie of the Eastern Shoshone signed the Treaty of Fort Bridger. This treaty gave Washakie's followers a reservation in the Wind River Valley in Wyoming. Four years later, the Eastern Shoshone lost a large portion of that land. It turned out that some white settlers already had homes in the Indian territory. The government gave the Indians $25,000 instead of the land. Later, the Eastern Shoshone shared their small space with their traditional enemies, the Arapaho. It was the noble Washakie who permitted the Arapaho and some Sioux Indians to live in peace on the Wind River Reservation, saying that "they would not hurt the land by living on it."

The Northern Shoshone faced similar problems. They moved to the Fort Hall Reservation in Southeastern Idaho in 1867. White settlers forced neighboring Bannock Indians onto the same land, making the reservation very crowded. Nevertheless, the government whittled away at the Indians' land as more and more white families moved into the area. Competition with these settlers for resources made it hard for the Shoshone to gather food for their families.

The white settlers surrounding Fort Hall added insult to injury throughout the 1870s. According to an 1873 treaty, the Fort Hall Indians were permitted to fish and forage on nearby lands outside their reservation to get what they needed. As the whites closed in on these lands, however, they destroyed the edible plants and the waterways. In 1878, the Bannock and Shoshone peoples expressed their growing anger in a series of violent attacks on the settlers. The Bannock

*Before and after: a young Shoshone man named Pat Tyhee in his traditional garb (left), and sporting the haircut and suit of a white man to show his acceptance of Christianity (right).*

War, which was quickly put down, resulted in more Indian than white deaths.

After the Bannock War, the government insisted that the Northern and Bannock Shoshone learn how to farm, but then failed

to give them tools and seeds. The Indians came close to starvation as a result.

The Western Shoshone were also mistreated. After a large Shoshone farm was established in 1877, white settlers claimed the land for themselves. That same year, the Duck Valley Reservation was established on the Idaho-Nevada border. This reservation lay outside of traditional Western Shoshone territory, so many tribe members did not wish to move there. Those who did were charged a lot of money for farming supplies, then paid very little in return for their crops.

Desperate, many Shoshone left their reservations and returned to their old territories. Some worked in the mines. Others combined traditional foraging with seasonal work on farms. It became clear that the government's attempt to relocate the Indians was failing. At one point, fewer than 60 percent of all Great Basin Indians were actually living on reservations.

For many years, the government had been trying to destroy Native American culture. The administration of President Ulysses S. Grant tried to force the Indians to become Christians. Grant replaced the government agents on reservations with missionaries, who taught the people there about God and the Bible. Since many tribes already practiced their own religions, the missionaries did not succeed in converting all the Indians. President Grant did not want Shoshone children to learn about the customs of their parents and grandparents. He did not want them to speak their native language.

By the 1880s, it was clear that President Grant's policies had failed. But the government still wanted to prepare Native American children to live in the white world. The Shoshone resisted the government's urging them to send their children to school. In an 1892 speech, Commissioner of Indian Affairs John T. Morgan proposed forcing them to go. His low opinion of the Indians was clear when he said, "At Fort Hall in Idaho, where the Shoshones and the Bannacks [sic] are, there is a school population of about two hundred and fifty. The people are degraded. They wander about in the mountains. Their women do most of what little work is done. They live in a beastly way. (I use the term thoughtfully, I have seen it); and they are refusing to send their children to school."

Despite the poor treatment they received on government reservations, the Shoshone eventually settled on them in greater numbers. It was only a matter of time before these once-proud people became dependent on white agents at the reservations. These agents controlled all of the people's finances. The Indians waited for them to

provide seeds for planting and to take the reservation's crops to market. Under this system, the Indians would never get all the money they rightfully earned.

In 1887, the U.S. government adopted the Dawes Severalty Act. This legislation forced Native Americans to give up their rights to reservation land in exchange for full U.S. citizenship. They would be allotted land on an individual or family basis. The

*A Fort Hall Shoshone family surrounded by white onlookers in 1909. The fact that mother and daughter wear traditional clothing, while father and son sport Euro-American attire, suggests that the government's success in stamping out Native American culture was far from complete.*

goal of the Act was to speed up the process of *assimilation*. But it actually worsened the plight of many Native Americans. Without tribal lands, entire groups became even more impoverished.

In response, the Shoshone—like many other native peoples—began to focus on spiritual concerns. A number of religious dances were created at this time: the Ghost Dance, the Bear Dance, and the Sun Dance. Perhaps the most popular was the Ghost Dance. The Shoshone and other tribes performed this dance to keep their hopes up. If they could endure the suffering of life on Earth, they believed that they would be reunited with the ghosts of their dead friends and relatives in the next world. The Bear Dance, too, was performed to help make reservation life more tolerable. The Sun Dance was performed to heal the sick and to alleviate their pain.

Shoshone life continued this way until the Presidency of Franklin Roosevelt. To combat the economic depression of the early 1930s, President Roosevelt brought about social reforms to improve Americans' lives. These reforms were called the New Deal. New Deal programs were designed to help Americans get jobs and avoid poverty. There was an "Indian New Deal" as well.

Roosevelt appointed a man named John Collier to be Commissioner of Indian Affairs. Collier worked hard to see that some past injustices were reversed. In some cases, land was returned to native groups. The Dawes Act was rescinded. Native Americans were now encouraged to preserve their culture by passing it on to their children.

The Tribal Reorganization Act of 1934 provided guidelines for Indian self-government. Reservation Indians would elect tribal councils and tribal chairmen. This way, the Shoshone and other groups would no longer be subject to the unfair rules and prejudices of federal reservation agents. The United States government again said its goal was to help tribes become self-sufficient. But the Shoshone had reason to suspect the government's motives in helping them. To make sure they were not taken advantage of, they needed strong leadership.

Unfortunately, there were few well-known Shoshone leaders by this time. Chief Washakie and the other great chiefs of the 1800s had already died. On the reservations, no one had risen to replace them because life there had deprived the Shoshone of traditional paths to leadership such as skill in hunting or warfare. But they persevered despite their lack of tribal leadership. The government provided extra money for farming. Sheep-raising cooperatives were formed at the Duck Valley, Fort Hall, and Wind River reservations.

Slowly, the Indian New Deal began to show some results. In 1935, the Wind River Shoshone sued the government for treaty violations and won money. Improved health care resulted in fewer cases of tuberculosis and other contagious diseases, which had taken a deadly toll on the Shoshone since their first contact with Europeans. More babies born on reservations survived infancy. The Shoshone population began to increase: the birth rate exceeded the death rate for the first time in decades.

Sadly, World War II brought an end to the New Deal, and with it, an end to the improved treatment of native peoples. Soon after the war, the government decided that it should stop protecting Native Americans on reservations. The Shoshone and other native groups fought this new policy. When asked to prepare their "termination plans," they refused.

As part of the termination process, the U.S. Claims Commission was established. This commission was supposed to award money to Indians in exchange for their reservation land. The stated reason for this switch in policy was to integrate Native Americans into the economy as farmers, merchants, and workers. A report by the Claims Commission, however, suggested another reason: the report noted that settling land claims would allow "proper development of the public domain."

In response, many of the reservation Shoshone made leasing arrangements with non-Indian fuel companies. Coal, oil, gas, uranium, phosphates, and other non-renewable natural resources are abundant in the Great Basin. Large leases were negotiated for oil and gas at Wind River and for phosphates at Fort Hall. In 1956, Wind River earned $1.3 million from mineral leasing. This figure increased steadily over the next two decades. Oil and gas payments became the major source of income for the reservation. In contrast, Fort Hall had received only $150,000 from its mineral leases by 1967.

In the latter half of the 20th century, control over Indian policy has shifted to individual states. In 1975, Congress passed the Indian Self-Determination Act, which gave tribes more decision-making power and encouraged their participation in writing

*The buffalo image in a wall mural appears to look on as students from Nevada's Reno-Sparks Indian Colony display their artwork. Today, Shoshone children learn both modern skills and age-old traditions.*

federal policies that affected them.

But the exploitation of their land by American corporations and the government still threatened to put an end to the Shoshone's way of life forever. Harvesting piñon nuts had always been a central part of Shoshone culture. After World War II, the government began to cut down vast areas of piñon forest in the Great Basin. The plan was to clear the land for crops. From 1962 to 1970, over one third of a million acres of piñon and juniper woodlands in Utah and Nevada were cut down by the National Forest Service and the Bureau of Land Management.

The destruction of the piñon forests angered many Shoshone men and women. They protested to the federal government. They cited treaty violations and spoke of the destruction of their age-old culture. Many Shoshone joined forces with other frustrated Native Americans. They formed a group called the American Indian Movement (AIM). In 1972, AIM organized a demonstration in Washington, D.C. This demonstration, known as the Trail of Broken Treaties, called attention to the government's long record of mistreating Indians.

Another ongoing concern of the Shoshone is nuclear testing. Since 1951, the Department of Defense has tested nuclear weapons in Western Shoshone territory. It is not known just how dangerous this testing has been to the environment—or to the people themselves.

Despite many hardships, the Shoshone have tried very hard to preserve their culture and heritage. Native voices have emerged in newspapers such as the *Wind River Journal* and the *Sho-Ban News*. Shoshone writers have published tribal histories. Oral historians have videotaped older Shoshone men and women telling stories they heard around the fires of piñon villages when they were children. These tapes are viewed by children in reservation schools taught by Shoshone teachers.

The people of the Great Basin have adjusted to the rapid pace of change in their culture during the 20th century. But they have not forgotten their traditions. Though they live in the modern world, they also teach their children the Shoshone language. The same adaptability that helped them thrive in the forbidding Great Basin will help insure the Shoshone's survival as a strong and independent people for years to come. ▲

# GLOSSARY

**assimilation**    the process of being absorbed into another culture

**chuckwalla**    a large lizard living in desert regions of the southwestern United States

**climate**    the weather conditions of a particular area, measured by temperature, annual rainfall, and wind

**conquistadors**    leaders of the Spanish conquest of North and South America during the 16th century

**ecology**    the relationships between people, animals, plants, and the environment in a given area

**herbalist**    a healer who treats diseases and injuries with plant remedies

**incantation**    a magical chant or song

**Louisiana Purchase**    the U.S. purchase of the region west of the Missouri River from France in 1803; the transaction doubled America's size and prompted the Lewis and Clark expedition

**mano**    a heavy, loaf-shaped stone used to grind food

**mortar**    a stone or wooden bowl in which food is pounded into meal

**nomadic**    traveling from place to place to obtain food and resources

**oral tradition**    a way of transmitting and preserving ideas through the spoken word, rather than through a written language

**pemmican**    a Native American food made out of dried meat ground into a powder and mixed with melted fat and berries

**piñon**    a low-growing type of pine tree in the western United States that bears edible seeds

**pith**    the spongy tissue inside some plant stalks

**prejudice**    unfair suspicion or hatred of a particular group, race, or religion

**reservation**    a tract of land retained by Native Americans for their own occupation and use

| | |
|---|---|
| rites of passage | rituals that mark changes in a person's life, such as reaching adulthood or marriage |
| shaman | a priest who uses magic to see the unknown, to control events, or to heal the sick |
| supernatural | of or relating to a world beyond the visible universe; the magical or spiritual |
| taboos | rules against certain behaviors, which are intended to protect people from supernatural harm |
| vision quest | a sacred ritual in which a person fasts and prays alone for several days, awaiting visions from the spirit world |
| weir | a gate set across a river to trap fish |

# CHRONOLOGY

c. 1700    Native Americans living east of the Rocky Mountains—including some Shoshone—organize their hunting and military activities around horses.

c. 1788    Sacajawea is born in northern Shoshone territory.

1803    President Thomas Jefferson buys land west of the Missouri River from France for $16 million.

1804–5    The Corps of Discovery, the Lewis and Clark expedition, explores the new U.S. territory, seeking a waterway to the Pacific Ocean. The Corps reaches the Pacific with Sacajawea as its guide.

1828–29    British fur trader Peter Ogden Skene discovers the Humboldt River in Nevada.

1847    Mormons settle in Salt Lake Valley in Utah and attempt to form their own nation of Deseret.

1848    Treaty of Guadalupe Hidalgo transfers land in Salt Lake Valley from Mexico to America. Gold is discovered in California.

1857    Miners bound for California are killed by Mormons in Utah during mounting conflicts over the treatment of Great Basin natives.

1859    The opening of gold and silver mines at the Comstock Lode in Nevada ushers in more white settlers.

1869    President Ulysses S. Grant elected; he enacts policies to eradicate traditional Native American cultures and religions.

1887    The Dawes Severalty Act divides tribal lands into privately owned allotments.

1934    The Tribal Reorganization Act, passed as part of President Roosevelt's "Indian New Deal," gives tribes more control over their own affairs.

1972    The American Indian Movement (AIM) organizes a cross-country caravan, ending in a demonstration in Washington, D.C., called the Trail of Broken Treaties.

1975    The Indian Self-Determination Act gives tribes more control over their local laws and more input in making government policies.

# FURTHER READING

Dramer, Kim. *The Shoshone*. Philadelphia: Chelsea House Publishers, 1997.

Madsen, Brigham D. *The Shoshoni Frontier and the Bear River Massacre*. Salt Lake City: University of Utah Press, 1985.

McKinney, Whitney. *A History of the Shoshone-Paiutes of the Duck Valley Reservation*. Salt Lake City: Howe Brothers, 1982.

Mooney, Martin J. *The Comanche Indians*. New York: Chelsea House Publishers, 1993.

Sherrow, Victoria. *Indians of the Plateau and Great Basin*. New York: Benford Books, Inc., 1992.

Time-Life Books. *People of the Western Range*. Alexandria, Va.: Time-Life Books, 1995.

# INDEX

## ABOUT THE AUTHOR

NATHANIEL MOSS graduated from Brown University with a B.A. in American Civilization. After completing a journalism internship with *Nation* magazine, he served as a speechwriter for the late U.S. representative Ted Weiss of New York. Moss is currently a freelance writer living in New York City. His other books include biographies of Ron Kovic, Humphrey Bogart, and W. E. B. Du Bois.

## Picture Credits